Essential Preparation for

UMAT

UNDERGRADUATE MEDICINE & HEALTH SCIENCES ADMISSION TEST

Series One

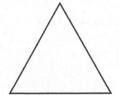  **3**

BOOK 3
NON-VERBAL REASONING

Mohan Dhall

Five Senses Education Pty Ltd
2/195 Prospect Highway
Seven Hills 2147
New South Wales
Australia

Dhall, Mohan
Book 3 - Non-Verbal Reasoning

ISBN 978-1-74130-773-3

CONTENTS

UMAT Trial Examination

Total Test Time: 180 minutes

- **Section 1: 48 Questions (70 minutes)**

- **Section 2: 44 Questions (55 minutes)**

- **Section 3: 42 Questions (55 minutes)**

This book covers Section 3

Section 3 – Non-Verbal Reasoning (55 minutes)

Questions in this section may be of several kinds. All are based on patterns or sequences of shapes and are designed to assess your ability to reason in the abstract and to solve problems in non-verbal contexts.

Section 3 - Non Verbal Reasoning

Question 1

Select the alternative that most logically and simply continues the series.

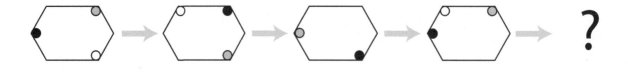

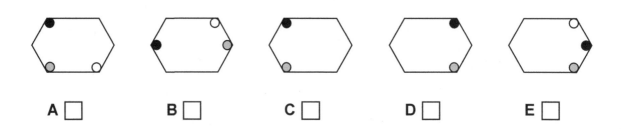

A ☐　　B ☐　　C ☐　　D ☐　　E ☐

Question 2

Select the alternative that most logically and simply continues the series.

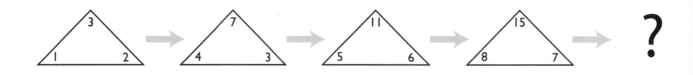

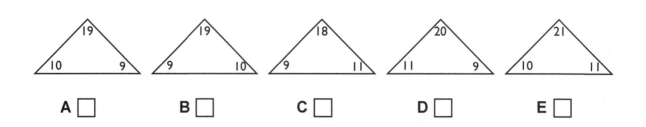

A ☐　　B ☐　　C ☐　　D ☐　　E ☐

Section 3 - Non Verbal Reasoning

Question 3

Select the alternative that most logically and simply continues the series.

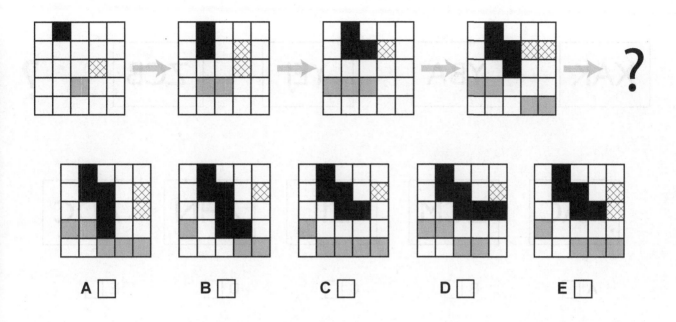

A	B	C	D	E

Question 4

Select the alternative that most logically and simply continues the series.

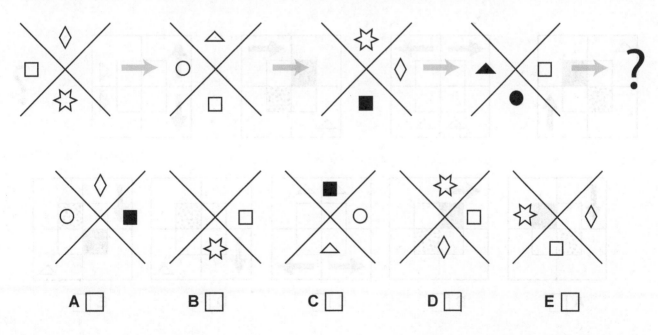

A	B	C	D	E

Section 3 - Non Verbal Reasoning

Question 5

Select the alternative that most logically and simply continues the series.

XAK → YBA → YEJ → ZCB → ?

XAC	ZCM	ZII	ZHN	ADC
A ☐	B ☐	C ☐	D ☐	E ☐

Question 6

Select the alternative that most logically and simply continues the series.

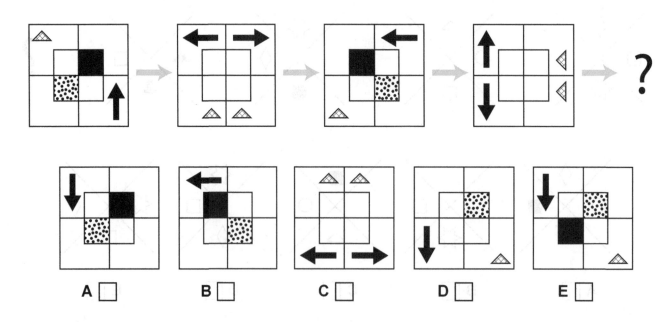

Section 3 - Non Verbal Reasoning

Question 7

Select the alternative that most logically and simply continues the series.

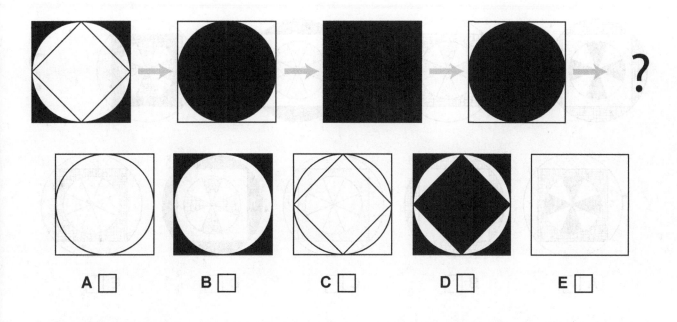

Question 8

Select the alternative that most logically and simply continues the series.

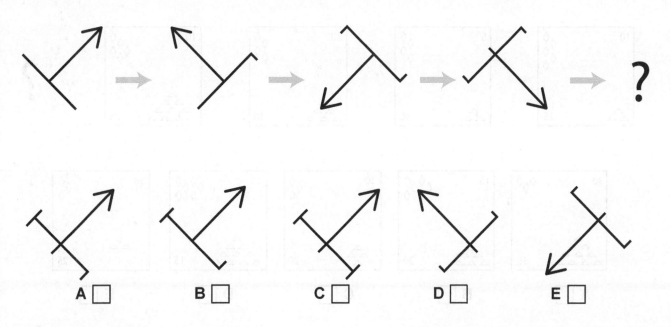

Section 3 - Non Verbal Reasoning

Question 9

Select the alternative that most logically and simply continues the series.

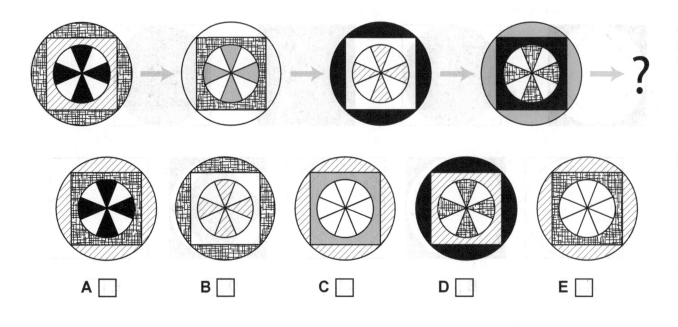

Question 10

Select the alternative that most logically and simply continues the series.

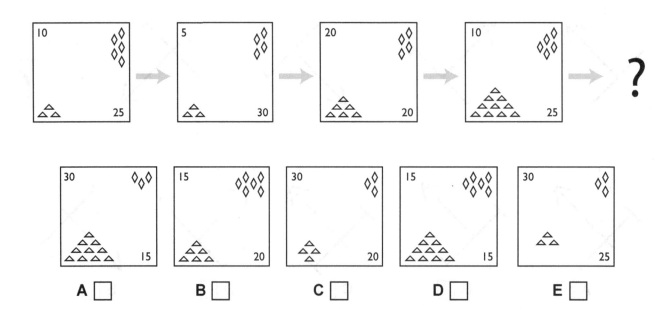

Section 3 - Non Verbal Reasoning

Question 11

Select the alternative that most logically and simply continues the series.

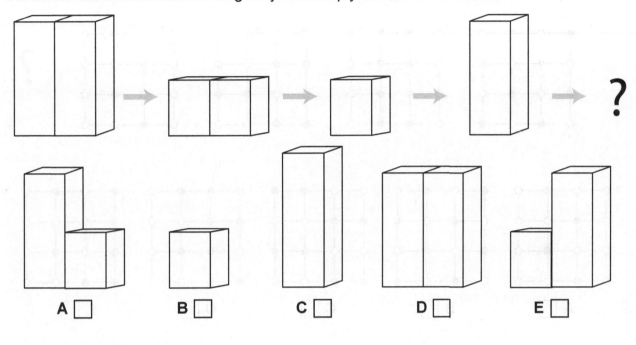

A ☐   B ☐   C ☐   D ☐   E ☐

Question 12

Select the alternative that most logically and simply continues the series.

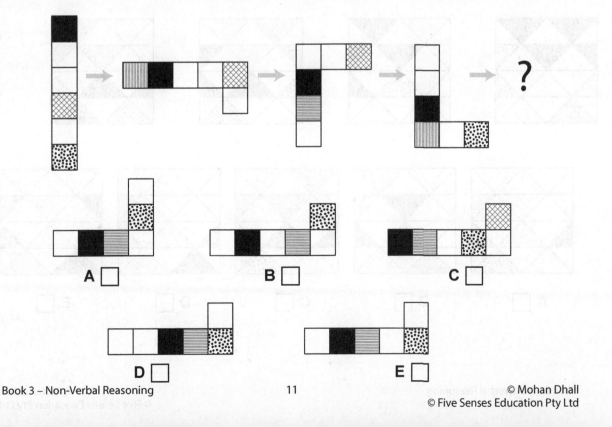

A ☐   B ☐   C ☐

D ☐   E ☐

Section 3 - Non Verbal Reasoning

Question 13

Select the alternative that most logically and simply continues the series.

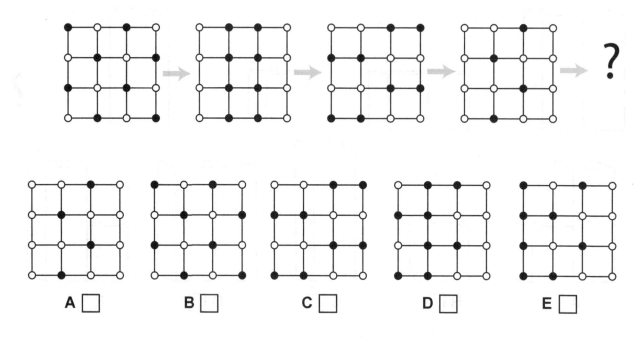

Question 14

Select the alternative that most logically and simply continues the series.

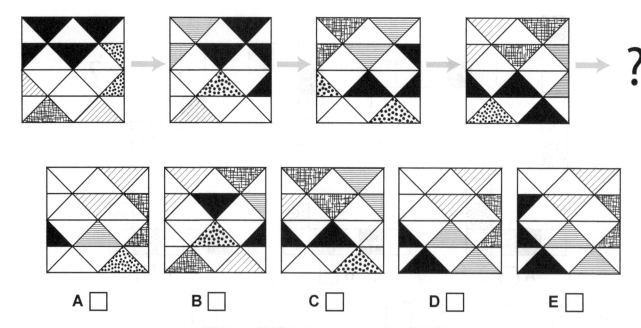

Section 3 - Non Verbal Reasoning

Question 15

Select the alternative that most logically and simply completes the picture.

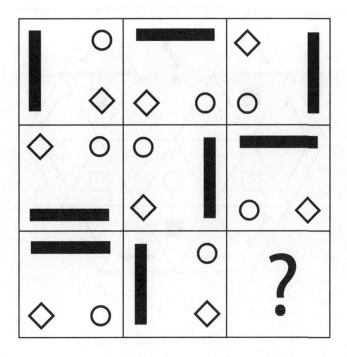

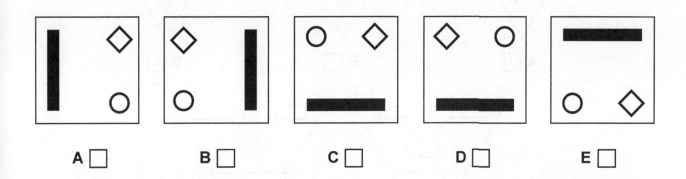

A ☐   **B** ☐   **C** ☐   **D** ☐   **E** ☐

Section 3 - Non Verbal Reasoning

Question 16

Select the alternative that most logically and simply completes the picture.

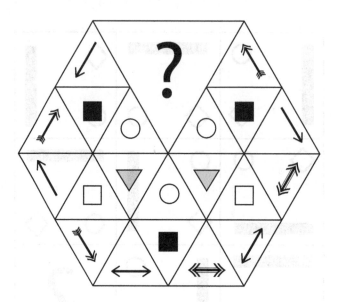

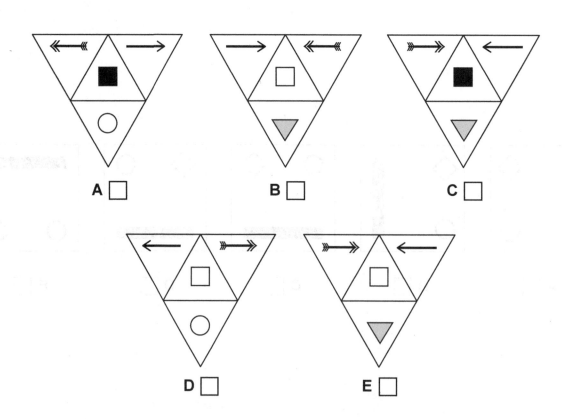

Section 3 - Non Verbal Reasoning

Question 17

Select the alternative that most logically and simply completes the picture.

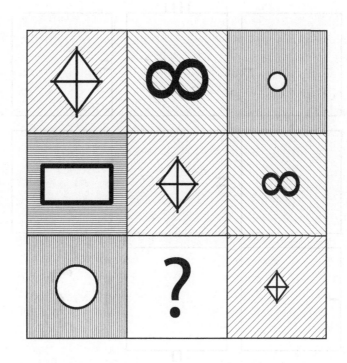

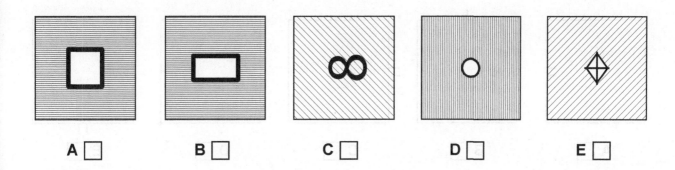

A ☐   B ☐   C ☐   D ☐   E ☐

Section 3 - Non Verbal Reasoning

Question 18

Select the alternative that most logically and simply completes the picture.

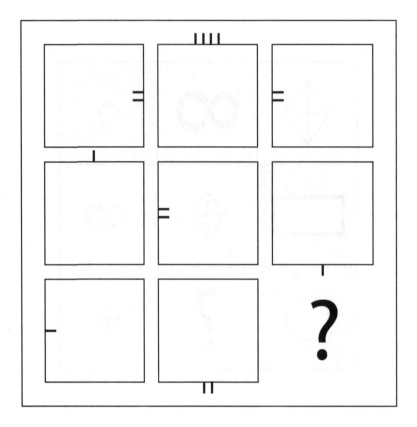

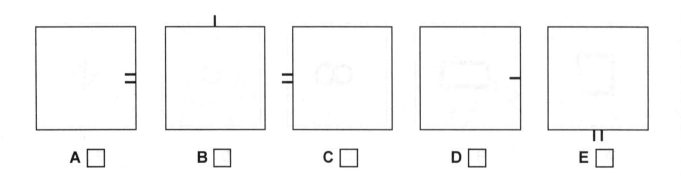

A ☐   B ☐   C ☐   D ☐   E ☐

Section 3 - Non Verbal Reasoning

Question 19

Select the alternative that most logically and simply completes the picture.

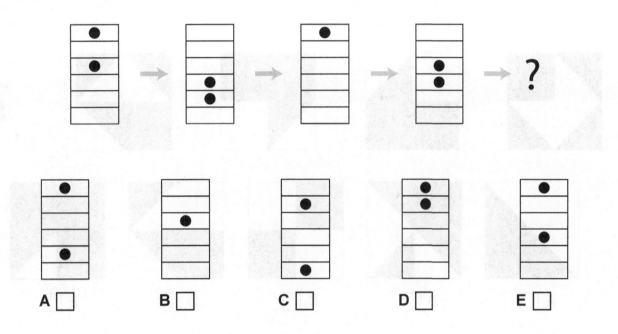

A ☐　　B ☐　　C ☐　　D ☐　　E ☐

Question 20

Select the alternative that most logically and simply completes the picture.

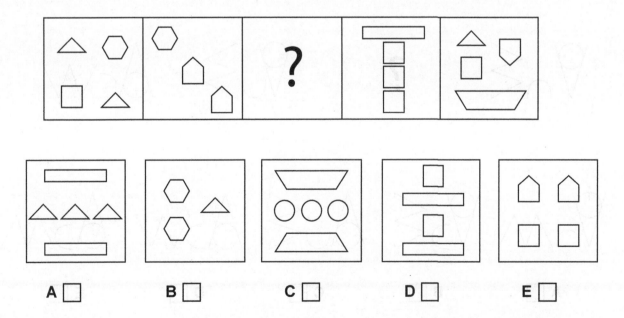

A ☐　　B ☐　　C ☐　　D ☐　　E ☐

© Mohan Dhall
© Five Senses Education Pty Ltd

Section 3 - Non Verbal Reasoning

Question 21

Select the alternative that most logically and simply completes the picture.

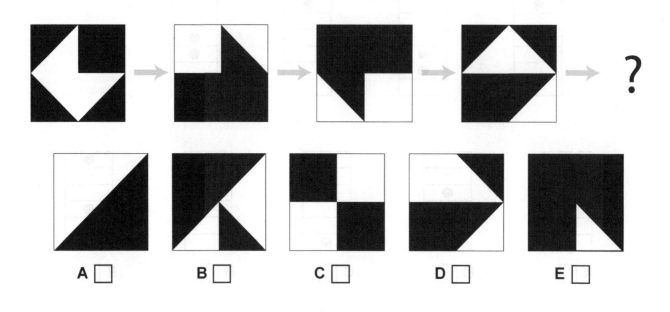

Question 22

Select the alternative that most logically and simply completes the picture.

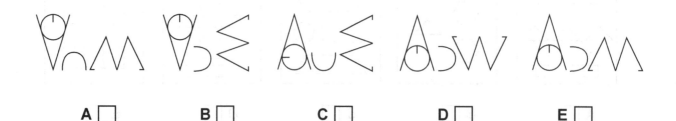

Section 3 - Non Verbal Reasoning

Question 23

Select the alternative that most logically and simply completes the picture.

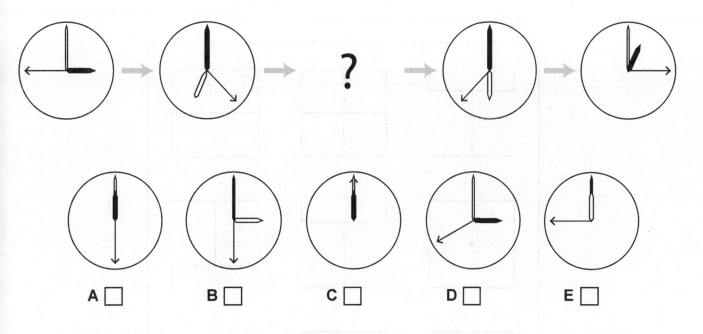

A ☐   B ☐   C ☐   D ☐   E ☐

Section 3 - Non Verbal Reasoning

Question 24

Select the alternative that most logically and simply completes the picture.

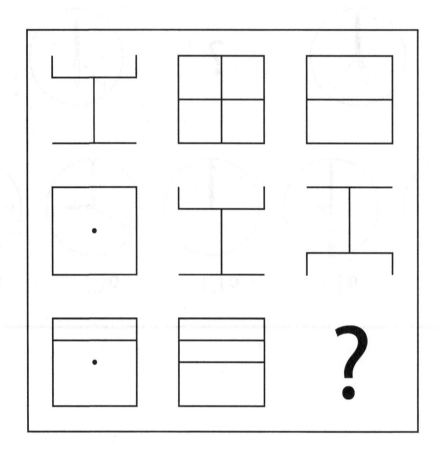

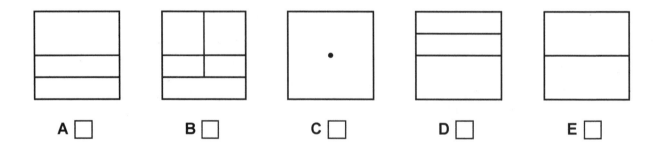

A ☐　　　B ☐　　　C ☐　　　D ☐　　　E ☐

Section 3 - Non Verbal Reasoning

Question 25

Select the alternative that most logically and simply completes the picture.

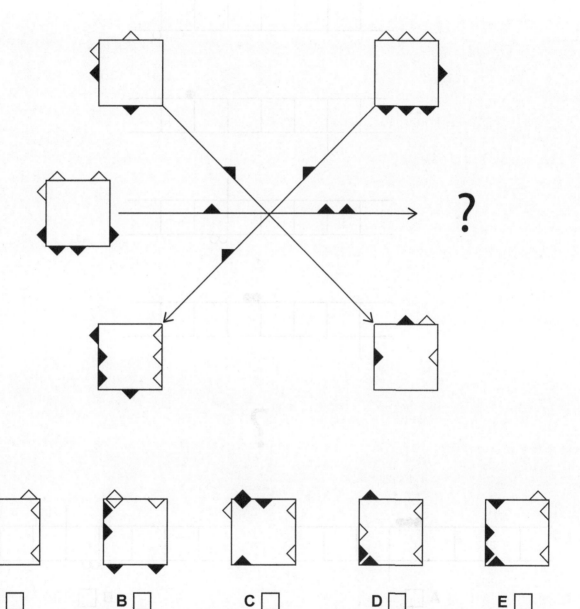

A ☐   B ☐   C ☐   D ☐   E ☐

Section 3 - Non Verbal Reasoning

Question 26

Select the alternative that most logically and simply completes the picture.

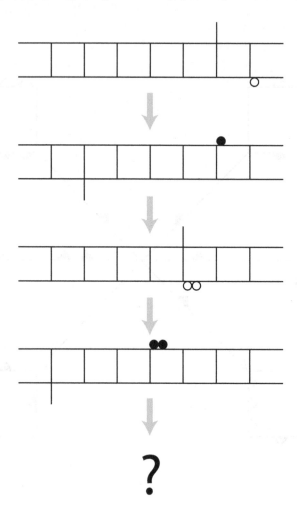

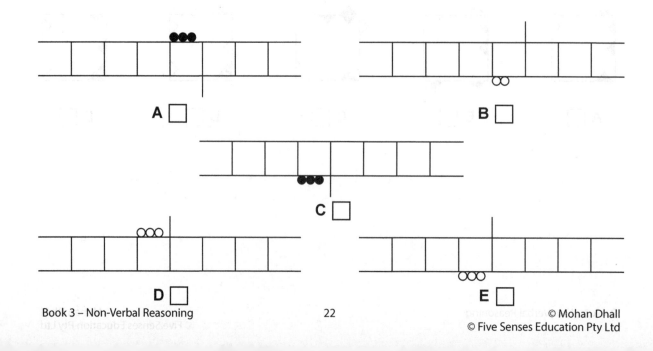

Section 3 - Non Verbal Reasoning

Question 27

Select the alternative that most logically and simply completes the picture.

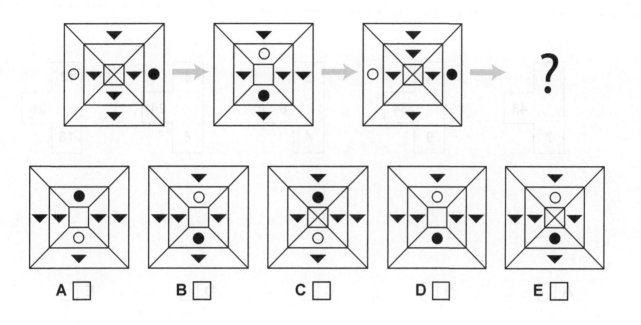

Question 28

Select the alternative that most logically and simply completes the picture.

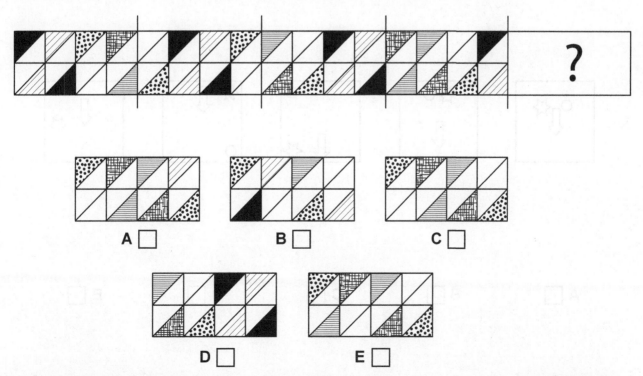

Section 3 - Non Verbal Reasoning

In the questions below, the five figures can be rearranged to form a logical sequence.
Select the alternative that would most logically and simply be in the <u>middle</u> of the sequence.

Question 29

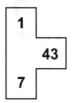 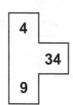 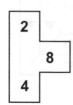 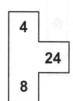 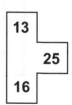

A ☐   B ☐   C ☐   D ☐   E ☐

Question 30

   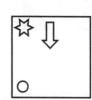

A ☐   B ☐   C ☐   D ☐   E ☐

Section 3 - Non Verbal Reasoning

In the questions below, the five figures can be rearranged to form a logical sequence. Select the alternative that would most logically and simply be in the <u>middle</u> of the sequence.

Question 31

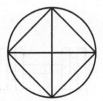 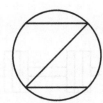 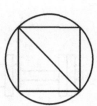 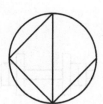

A ☐   B ☐   C ☐   D ☐   E ☐

Question 32

MQJPA   NAJPT   NQJPA   MQJSA   NAJPA

A ☐   B ☐   C ☐   D ☐   E ☐

Section 3 - Non Verbal Reasoning

In the questions below, the five figures can be rearranged to form a logical sequence. Select the alternative that would most logically and simply be in the <u>middle</u> of the sequence.

Question 33

A ☐   B ☐   C ☐   D ☐   E ☐

Question 34

   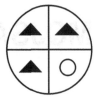         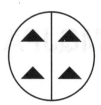

A ☐   B ☐   C ☐   D ☐   E ☐

Section 3 - Non Verbal Reasoning

In the questions below, the five figures can be rearranged to form a logical sequence.
Select the alternative that would most logically and simply be in the <u>middle</u> of the sequence.

Question 35

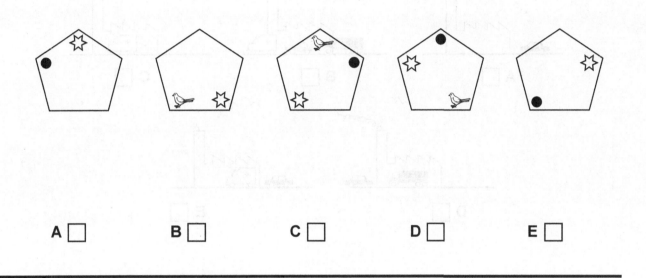

A ☐   B ☐   C ☐   D ☐   E ☐

Question 36

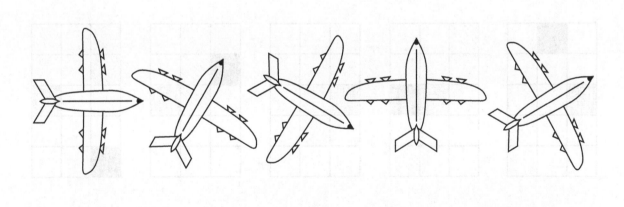

A ☐   B ☐   C ☐   D ☐   E ☐

Section 3 - Non Verbal Reasoning

In the questions below, the five figures can be rearranged to form a logical sequence. Select the alternative that would most logically and simply be in the <u>middle</u> of the sequence.

Question 37

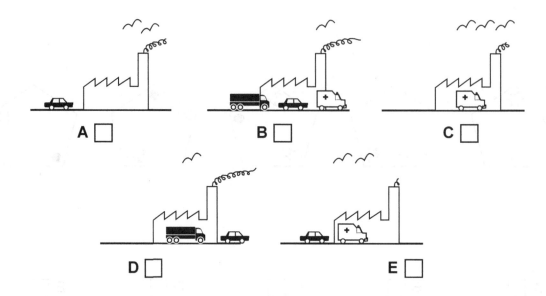

Question 38

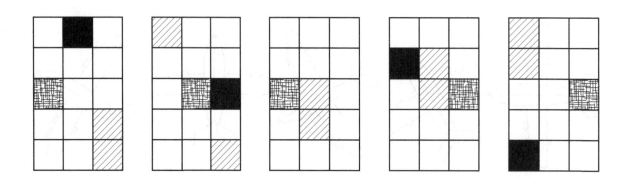

A ☐   B ☐   C ☐   D ☐   E ☐

Section 3 - Non Verbal Reasoning

In the questions below, the five figures can be rearranged to form a logical sequence. Select the alternative that would most logically and simply be in the <u>middle</u> of the sequence.

Question 39

A ☐   B ☐   C ☐   D ☐   E ☐

Question 40

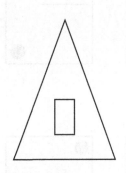 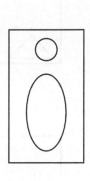 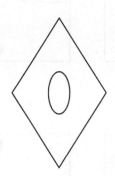 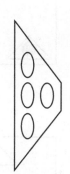 

A ☐   B ☐   C ☐   D ☐   E ☐

Section 3 - Non Verbal Reasoning

In the questions below, the five figures can be rearranged to form a logical sequence. Select the alternative that would most logically and simply be in the <u>middle</u> of the sequence.

Question 41

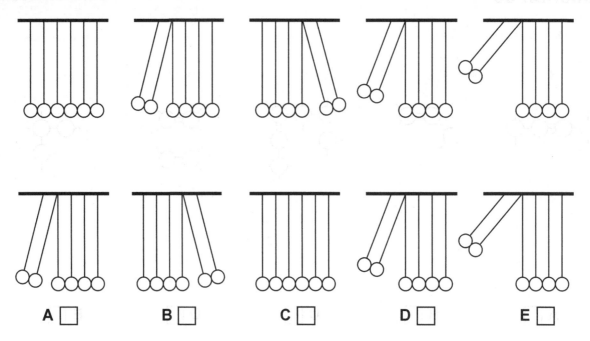

A ☐   B ☐   C ☐   D ☐   E ☐

Question 42

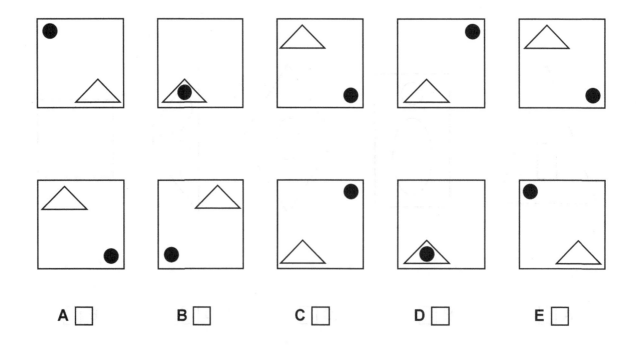

A ☐   B ☐   C ☐   D ☐   E ☐

ANSWERS
Summary & Worked Solutions
Multiple Choice Answer Sheet

Summary of Answers

Question 1	D	Question 12	E	Question 23	C	Question 34	A
Question 2	B	Question 13	A	Question 24	A	Question 35	C
Question 3	C	Question 14	C	Question 25	A	Question 36	E
Question 4	B	Question 15	C	Question 26	E	Question 37	A
Question 5	C	Question 16	E	Question 27	B	Question 38	B
Question 6	E	Question 17	B	Question 28	C	Question 39	D
Question 7	B	Question 18	D	Question 29	D	Question 40	B
Question 8	B	Question 19	A	Question 30	A	Question 41	A
Question 9	C	Question 20	D	Question 31	E	Question 42	A
Question 10	A	Question 21	B	Question 32	C		
Question 11	D	Question 22	E	Question 33	D		

Answers with fully worked solutions

<u>Note:</u>

Questions 1 – 14 involve test-takers selecting the alternative that most logically continues the series.

Questions 15 – 28 involve test-takers completing the picture.

Questions 29 – 42 involve test-takers placing five pictures into a logical sequence and then selecting the middle picture from the correct sequence.

Question 1

D

The black dot goes clockwise two spaces at a time. The white dot also goes clockwise but three positions at a time. When the white dot overlaps with any other dot it cannot be seen, hence in the third picture in the sequence it is not shown. In the third picture the white and black dots occupy the same position and thus only the black dot can be seen. The grey dot goes clockwise two positions at a time. Hence D is correct

Question 2

B

The sum of the numbers in the corners of the base of the triangle equals the number at the apex. As each successive triangle has the base numbers increasing by 1 each, the total at the apex goes up by 4. Thus the top number must be 19. However, the numbers along the base also reverse position, thus the odd and even numbers keep swapping sides. Thus, the 9 must be in the bottom left hand corner, hence the answer is B.

Question 3

C

The black squares increase in length by one in successive patterns. They also follow the rule 'one down, one across'. This means the only correct answers must be C or E. The light grey square follows the pattern 'up one, lose one' then 'across one, lose one'. Thus C is correct for this sequence. The dark grey boxes increase in length by one but upon hitting the side the whole sequence moves across and scrolls downwards by one row.

Question 4

B

There are two patterns alternating here, which makes it tricky. The first, third and fifth are related, and the second and fourth are related. Hence, look at what is occurring between the first and third of the patterns and use this to determine what the fifth would be. The diamond moves clockwise by one space and the square moves counter-clockwise by one space and changes colour. The star will alternate moving between the bottom position and the top position. The diamond therefore should occupy the bottom position, as should the star. The square should be white and should be in the right-hand position. Since the star and diamond both occupy the same space the diamond cannot be seen - only the star. Hence B is correct.

Question 5

C

In this question there are two patterns of letters that are alternating. Thus the first, third and fifth patterns will be related. Separately, the second, fourth and sixth are related. Thus, look carefully at the relationship between the first and third boxes. Here it can be seen that X becomes Y, the next letter in the alphabet. Thus, in the fifth box the first letter should be Z. The middle letter A in the first box becomes E – a separation of three letters, but also the next vowel. This means that in the fifth box the middle letter should be I (a separation of three letters and also the next vowel). The third letter K becomes a J, moving backwards in the alphabet by one place. Thus the third letter should be I in the fifth box. Thus C is the correct answer.

Question 6

E

There is a sequence of alternate patterns occurring in this question. Thus, the first, third and fifth boxes are related and the second, fourth and sixth are also related. The relationship between the first and third boxes is that the triangle is moving counter clockwise by one square each time and the arrow is also moving counter clockwise one space at a time. This movement is repeated by the black squares and the dotted squares that are moving counter clockwise. Thus the correct answer is E.

Question 7

B

There are three shapes: a diamond, a circle and a square, in that order. Each of them is being moved from top to bottom and then makes its way back to the top. Each also changes colour from black to white to black. When the diamond moves back it cannot be seen as it is covered by the square. This is also the case with the circle. Thus, in the third picture the black square is obscuring a white diamond and a white circle. The fifth pattern in the sequence must be the white square becoming black, the white diamond becoming black (and moving to the bottom) and the black circle becoming white and moving to the top. Thus B is correct.

Question 8

B

Here the shape is rotating counter clockwise by 90º at a time. Further, a line is added to the base of the shape on successive rotations. These lines are moving from above the base to below the base and vice versa on successive rotations. Thus, in the fifth shape the arrow must be pointing as it was in the starting position (a rotation of 90º counter clockwise). The middle line must move over the arrow and one of the ends will get another line. The other end will swap sides, hence B is correct.

Question 9

C

All of the shapes go through a succession of changes in pattern. These changes are black to grey to angled-lines to hashed and then white. The sequence of patterns then restarts. This means that the grey circle should become angled-lines, the black square should become grey and the hashed start should become white. This arrangement is shown in C.

Question 10

A

Here there are two patterns occurring one relating to the first, third and fifth arrangements and the other to the second and fourth. In the case of the first and third squares we can see that top left-hand 10 has become 20 and that the bottom right-hand 25 has become 20. Following the mathematical pattern should mean the next square in this series would have the 20 becoming a 30 in left-hand top corner and the 20 would become 15. This means that A should be correct, but it needs to be confirmed by checking the other shapes. The 5 diamonds in the first square becomes 4 diamonds and then should become 3 diamonds. Similarly, the 3 triangles becomes 6 and then 10. Hence A is indeed correct.

Question 11

D

Here the volume halves successively. Thereafter it doubles. So, if it halves once and then halves again, then when it doubles it should double again. Hence double the fourth shape is two of such a shape which is represented by D.

Question 12

E

All of the squares move along by one space at a time. This can be seen by following black square which can be seen moving along by one square at a time. It can be seen that the lined square follows the black square and that a white square follows these two, then the dotted square. This sequence of shapes is maintained in E. Note an overlap is the rotation of the shapes through 90° clockwise.

Question 13

A

This is a tricky question! It looks like all the dots may be moving but on closer inspection it will be realised that the middle dots in the first box never actually move. Keeping the middle two column of dots fixed now see what is happening to the other dots. It can be seen that the top row dot in the left corner moves right one space and the second row dot on the right-hand side moves left one space. This is repeated in the lower rows. In the third picture the dots have continued their move but this time have been displaced by two spaces. In the fourth picture the dots have moved three places but in the next row down (or in the case of the bottom row – back to the top). Thus, the next move should be by four places giving A.

Question 14

D

The top two rows are moving right by one space at a time and the bottom two rows are moving left by one space at a time. The pattern of triangles is black, followed by lines, followed by hashed and then angled lines. The next triangle is blank. After the blank triangles is the dotted triangle and then the pattern repeats. This is represented by box D.

Question 15

C

The shapes in the top row are rotating clockwise by one space at a time. The shapes in the second row are rotating counter clockwise by one space at a time. The shapes in the third row are also rotating counter clockwise and thus C is correct.

Question 16

E

The circles and gray triangles are alternating and thus the missing inner shape must be a grey triangle. This eliminates A and D. The squares alternate black and white and thus the square must be white. Thus C is eliminated. The arrows are therefore the key. Starting on the left-hand side and going counter clockwise, it can be seen that the single arrow reverses direction and then doubles. The whole sequence then "unwinds". Thus, the outward facing arrows in the top right-hand triangle must become inwards facing.

Question 17

B

The key to this is to look at the diagonals. It can be seen that the infinity symbols gets smaller as it goes down to the right. Similarly following the top left-hand kites downwards and to the right it can be seen that they reduce in size on each row. The pattern must then follow with the rectangle getting smaller to the right and thus the correct answer is B.

Question 18

D

Here there is a subtraction pattern. This is complicated by two further patterns. The first is the rotation counter clockwise moving down the columns. The second is the placement of the lines alternating from outside to inside the square and from inside to outside the square. Thus, following the right-hand column downwards there should be one line. Following the rotation the line should be on the right-hand side of the square. Following the inside-outside pattern the line should be inside the square. Thus D is correct.

Question 19

A

The top dot moves down by three places at a time (rotating to the top once it reaches the bottom) whereas the second dot goes down by two spaces at a time. When they are in the same square we can only see one dot. Thus the correct answer is A.

Question 20

D

Here the key is the sum of the sides. Circles are counted as 1, triangles 3, squares, rectangles and quadrilaterals 4, pentagons 5 and hexagons 6. The total sum of the sides of all of the shapes equals 16. Thus, D is correct.

Question 21

B

Here the shape is always three eighths white and five eighths black. The 'eighths' can be seen as triangles and it may help to 'draw' the lines in that create the triangles. The only shape with three eighths white is B.

Question 22

E

There are four distinct shapes to look at: a 'V', a circle with line inside, a 'U' shape and a summation symbol: Σ

The V moves 180° at a time. The circle is rotating counter clockwise by 90° at a time. The other two shapes are both rotating 90° at a time clockwise. Thus, the correct answer is E.

Question 23

C

Here there are several different things occurring. Firstly the hour hand and the minute hand are alternating between black and white. Secondly, the successive clock are increasing in time by 4 hours, 5 hours, 6 hours and 7 hours. Lastly, the second hand is moving 37.5 seconds each time around the clock. Thus, 7pm and 22.5 seconds will increase by 5 hours and the second hand will move 37.5 seconds to be exactly in line with the hour hands making the time 12.

Question 24

A

Here the boxes in the columns are adding downwards with the subtraction of any vertical shapes that are within the boxes. Thus the answer should have two horizontal lines – one at halfway and one a quarter way from the bottom. The vertical middle line disappears giving A.

Question 25

A

Firstly, the black triangles on the arrows indicate the number of outside triangles (usually) on the lower edge of the square that must come inside. Secondly, every white triangle on the upper edge goes inside the square. Thirdly, the square rotates clockwise by 90°. Applying this means that three black squares must come inside. Also, the rotation with the white squares coming in means only A and E are possible. But of these only A has three black triangles inside, whereas E has four. Hence, logically, A must be correct.

Question 26

E

There are two alternate patterns occurring here with the white balls and the black balls. The number of balls increases by one in each successive addition to the pattern. The balls move two places to the left. A further complication is the line that moves one space to the left for each of the successive patterns. Thus the correct answer must have three white balls and they must have moved two squares left. The extended line must move one space left giving E.

Question 27

B

The first thing to note is the middle square. This alternates from being crossed to blank, crossed to blank. Thus in the correct answer it must be blank. This eliminates C and E. Next look at the arrangement of triangles in the middle square. These triangles move to the outside square and rotate 90° counter clockwise. Then they come back into the middle square in the third picture in the sequence and rotate 90° counter clockwise again. This means that the next picture should have should have the triangles outside and rotated again as shown in B and E. But E is not correct, hence B must be correct. To confirm, now look at the remaining shapes. The circles go from outside to inside to outside. They therefore must go back into the middle square. They rotate 90° clockwise, the 90° counter clockwise, then 90° clockwise. Hence in the next picture they should look as they do in the second picture, having moved clockwise again. Thus B is correct.

© Mohan Dhall
© Five Senses Education Pty Ltd

Question 28

C

The top row of four triangles is moving right to left and the bottom row is moving left to right. The order of the pattern is black to angled lines to dots to hash to horizontal lines to white and then back to black. Following this for the top row means that the next triangle after the hash should be dotted. For the bottom row the next shade after the horizontal lines is cross hash.

This means that for the top row the pattern (left to right) will be dots, hash, horizontal lines and white. For the bottom row the pattern (left to right) will be white, horizontal lines, hash and dots – as shown in C.

Question 29

D

The pattern is quite tricky. The number to the right is the square of the difference of the numbers added to the number at the bottom. The sequence in order is $(4 - 2)^2 + 4$, $(16 - 13)^2 + 16$, $(8 - 4)^2 + 8$, $(9 - 4)^2 + 9$ and then $(7 - 1)^2 + 7$. Thus the sequence follows the squares. In order then the middle one is D.

Question 30

A

The ball is following an arc from the bottom left hand corner to the top right hand corner. The star is following an arc from the bottom right hand corner to the top left hand corner. The arrow is falling straight from top to bottom. Thus when the arrow is in the middle the objects are half way to the end point and half way from their staring positions as shown in A.

Question 31

E

Here the shape is adding a line each time. The sequence in order would be C, B, E, D and A. The middle line (diameter) is rotating counter clockwise by 45° each time as well. Thus the middle of the sequence must be E with 4 lines and rotated by 90°.

Question 32

C

One letter is changing each time. This means that the order of the sequence must be either MQJSA, MQJPA, NQJPA, NAJPA and NAJPT or this is exact reverse. Thus, NQJPA must be in the middle when the letters group is in order hence C is correct.

Question 33

D

Here the weight is increasing to a maximum then going back to what it was originally. Assume the large weights are 10kg and the smaller weights are 5 kg. This would mean that the barbell in A and B would carry 40kg and in C and E, 50 kg. The barbell in D carries 60kg and lies in the middle of the sequence.

Question 34

A

The sequence in order is C, D, A, E and B. The pattern is 3 white triangles and 1 black with two dividing lines. The next in the sequence is 2 white triangles and two black triangles (filling counter clockwise) with now only one dividing line. The third in the sequence must be three black triangles filling counter clockwise with no lines (A). It follows that the next would be fully black triangles with one line (E) and then the introduction of a new sequence with the white circle replacing one black triangle.

Question 35

C

The shapes are moving within the pentagon. The star is moving clockwise one position every time. The dot is moving clockwise 4 positions each time. The bird is moving clockwise 2 positions each time but will not appear when another shape and it occupy the same corner.

The sequence in order is: E, B, C, D and A with the middle picture in the sequence being C.

© Mohan Dhall
© Five Senses Education Pty Ltd

Question 36

E

The plane is being rotated from North to East South East (or 30° South of East), moving 30° at a time clockwise around the compass. Thus, the middle in the sequence must be the plane East North East or 30° North of East as in E

Question 37

A

The birds and the vehicles are distractors and are not relevant. Here the sequence depends on time as evidenced by the length of smoke blowing from the factory chimney. In time order the sequence must be E, C, A, B and D. Thus the middle picture must be A.

Question 38

B

There are three different moving sets of shapes. The angled line boxes are moving downwards to the right (ie down two across one) and scrolling from right to left. The black dot moves upwards to the right by one square each time. The Cross hatched square moves one square at a time from right to left (scrolling to the other side when it reaches the edge).

The correct sequence is E, C, B, D, A thus the middle pattern in the sequence is B.

Question 39

D

The key thing here is the number of bonds between the atoms. The distractor is the number of atoms. The number of bonds varies from 2 to 6, in order E (2), B (3), D (4), A (5) and C (6). Thus, looking at the number of bonds the middle in order is four as shown in D.

Question 40

B

The key here is to look at the number of sides in total, taking an oval as having one side and a circle as having one side. The number of sides varies from 4 (D) to 5 (C), 6 (B), 7 (A) and 8 (D). Thus, in order the middle number of sides is 6 and the correct answer is B.

© Mohan Dhall
© Five Senses Education Pty Ltd

Question 41

A

The Newton's Cradle works based on the principle of conservation of energy and momentum. Here the falling balls strike from the left and cause the balls on the right to swing outwards. The sequence begins with the balls high to the left and then falling with the fourth of the sequence being the impact and the fifth the movement of the right hand balls outwards. Thus the sequence in order is D, E, A, C and B.

The middle in the order is therefore A.

Question 42

A

The black dot is moving counter clockwise three spaces at a time. The triangle is moving counter clockwise one space at a time for two moves then clockwise for two moves.

Thus the sequence begins with the right most square, then the second from the right, then the left most square, then the second square from the left then the middle square. Using the letters the order is:

A, D, E, C and B – thus the middle in order is E.

Notes

Notes

Notes

Notes

Notes

Notes

49

Notes

Notes

Essential Preparation for

UMAT

UNDERGRADUATE MEDICINE & HEALTH SCIENCES ADMISSION TEST

MULTIPLE CHOICE ANSWER SHEET

1	Ⓐ Ⓑ Ⓒ Ⓓ Ⓔ					22	Ⓐ Ⓑ Ⓒ Ⓓ Ⓔ				
2	Ⓐ Ⓑ Ⓒ Ⓓ Ⓔ					23	Ⓐ Ⓑ Ⓒ Ⓓ Ⓔ				
3	Ⓐ Ⓑ Ⓒ Ⓓ Ⓔ					24	Ⓐ Ⓑ Ⓒ Ⓓ Ⓔ				
4	Ⓐ Ⓑ Ⓒ Ⓓ Ⓔ					25	Ⓐ Ⓑ Ⓒ Ⓓ Ⓔ				
5	Ⓐ Ⓑ Ⓒ Ⓓ Ⓔ					26	Ⓐ Ⓑ Ⓒ Ⓓ Ⓔ				
6	Ⓐ Ⓑ Ⓒ Ⓓ Ⓔ					27	Ⓐ Ⓑ Ⓒ Ⓓ Ⓔ				
7	Ⓐ Ⓑ Ⓒ Ⓓ Ⓔ					28	Ⓐ Ⓑ Ⓒ Ⓓ Ⓔ				
8	Ⓐ Ⓑ Ⓒ Ⓓ Ⓔ					29	Ⓐ Ⓑ Ⓒ Ⓓ Ⓔ				
9	Ⓐ Ⓑ Ⓒ Ⓓ Ⓔ					30	Ⓐ Ⓑ Ⓒ Ⓓ Ⓔ				
10	Ⓐ Ⓑ Ⓒ Ⓓ Ⓔ					31	Ⓐ Ⓑ Ⓒ Ⓓ Ⓔ				
11	Ⓐ Ⓑ Ⓒ Ⓓ Ⓔ					32	Ⓐ Ⓑ Ⓒ Ⓓ Ⓔ				
12	Ⓐ Ⓑ Ⓒ Ⓓ Ⓔ					33	Ⓐ Ⓑ Ⓒ Ⓓ Ⓔ				
13	Ⓐ Ⓑ Ⓒ Ⓓ Ⓔ					34	Ⓐ Ⓑ Ⓒ Ⓓ Ⓔ				
14	Ⓐ Ⓑ Ⓒ Ⓓ Ⓔ					35	Ⓐ Ⓑ Ⓒ Ⓓ Ⓔ				
15	Ⓐ Ⓑ Ⓒ Ⓓ Ⓔ					36	Ⓐ Ⓑ Ⓒ Ⓓ Ⓔ				
16	Ⓐ Ⓑ Ⓒ Ⓓ Ⓔ					37	Ⓐ Ⓑ Ⓒ Ⓓ Ⓔ				
17	Ⓐ Ⓑ Ⓒ Ⓓ Ⓔ					38	Ⓐ Ⓑ Ⓒ Ⓓ Ⓔ				
18	Ⓐ Ⓑ Ⓒ Ⓓ Ⓔ					39	Ⓐ Ⓑ Ⓒ Ⓓ Ⓔ				
19	Ⓐ Ⓑ Ⓒ Ⓓ Ⓔ					40	Ⓐ Ⓑ Ⓒ Ⓓ Ⓔ				
20	Ⓐ Ⓑ Ⓒ Ⓓ Ⓔ					41	Ⓐ Ⓑ Ⓒ Ⓓ Ⓔ				
21	Ⓐ Ⓑ Ⓒ Ⓓ Ⓔ					42	Ⓐ Ⓑ Ⓒ Ⓓ Ⓔ				

Essential Preparation for
UMAT

UNDERGRADUATE MEDICINE & HEALTH SCIENCES ADMISSION TEST

MULTIPLE CHOICE ANSWER SHEET

Use pencil when filling out this sheet

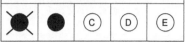

Fill in the circle correctly
● Ⓑ Ⓒ Ⓓ Ⓔ

If you make a mistake neatly cross it out and circle the correct response
⊗ ● Ⓒ Ⓓ Ⓔ

1 Ⓐ Ⓑ Ⓒ Ⓓ Ⓔ   22 Ⓐ Ⓑ Ⓒ Ⓓ Ⓔ

2 Ⓐ Ⓑ Ⓒ Ⓓ Ⓔ   23 Ⓐ Ⓑ Ⓒ Ⓓ Ⓔ

3 Ⓐ Ⓑ Ⓒ Ⓓ Ⓔ   24 Ⓐ Ⓑ Ⓒ Ⓓ Ⓔ

4 Ⓐ Ⓑ Ⓒ Ⓓ Ⓔ   25 Ⓐ Ⓑ Ⓒ Ⓓ Ⓔ

5 Ⓐ Ⓑ Ⓒ Ⓓ Ⓔ   26 Ⓐ Ⓑ Ⓒ Ⓓ Ⓔ

6 Ⓐ Ⓑ Ⓒ Ⓓ Ⓔ   27 Ⓐ Ⓑ Ⓒ Ⓓ Ⓔ

7 Ⓐ Ⓑ Ⓒ Ⓓ Ⓔ   28 Ⓐ Ⓑ Ⓒ Ⓓ Ⓔ

8 Ⓐ Ⓑ Ⓒ Ⓓ Ⓔ   29 Ⓐ Ⓑ Ⓒ Ⓓ Ⓔ

9 Ⓐ Ⓑ Ⓒ Ⓓ Ⓔ   30 Ⓐ Ⓑ Ⓒ Ⓓ Ⓔ

10 Ⓐ Ⓑ Ⓒ Ⓓ Ⓔ   31 Ⓐ Ⓑ Ⓒ Ⓓ Ⓔ

11 Ⓐ Ⓑ Ⓒ Ⓓ Ⓔ   32 Ⓐ Ⓑ Ⓒ Ⓓ Ⓔ

12 Ⓐ Ⓑ Ⓒ Ⓓ Ⓔ   33 Ⓐ Ⓑ Ⓒ Ⓓ Ⓔ

13 Ⓐ Ⓑ Ⓒ Ⓓ Ⓔ   34 Ⓐ Ⓑ Ⓒ Ⓓ Ⓔ

14 Ⓐ Ⓑ Ⓒ Ⓓ Ⓔ   35 Ⓐ Ⓑ Ⓒ Ⓓ Ⓔ

15 Ⓐ Ⓑ Ⓒ Ⓓ Ⓔ   36 Ⓐ Ⓑ Ⓒ Ⓓ Ⓔ

16 Ⓐ Ⓑ Ⓒ Ⓓ Ⓔ   37 Ⓐ Ⓑ Ⓒ Ⓓ Ⓔ

17 Ⓐ Ⓑ Ⓒ Ⓓ Ⓔ   38 Ⓐ Ⓑ Ⓒ Ⓓ Ⓔ

18 Ⓐ Ⓑ Ⓒ Ⓓ Ⓔ   39 Ⓐ Ⓑ Ⓒ Ⓓ Ⓔ

19 Ⓐ Ⓑ Ⓒ Ⓓ Ⓔ   40 Ⓐ Ⓑ Ⓒ Ⓓ Ⓔ

20 Ⓐ Ⓑ Ⓒ Ⓓ Ⓔ   41 Ⓐ Ⓑ Ⓒ Ⓓ Ⓔ

21 Ⓐ Ⓑ Ⓒ Ⓓ Ⓔ   42 Ⓐ Ⓑ Ⓒ Ⓓ Ⓔ

Essential Preparation for

UMAT

UNDERGRADUATE MEDICINE & HEALTH SCIENCES ADMISSION TEST

MULTIPLE CHOICE ANSWER SHEET

Use pencil when filling out this sheet

Fill in the circle correctly				
●	Ⓑ	Ⓒ	Ⓓ	Ⓔ

If you make a mistake neatly cross it out and circle the correct response				
⊗	●	Ⓒ	Ⓓ	Ⓔ

1 Ⓐ Ⓑ Ⓒ Ⓓ Ⓔ
2 Ⓐ Ⓑ Ⓒ Ⓓ Ⓔ
3 Ⓐ Ⓑ Ⓒ Ⓓ Ⓔ
4 Ⓐ Ⓑ Ⓒ Ⓓ Ⓔ
5 Ⓐ Ⓑ Ⓒ Ⓓ Ⓔ
6 Ⓐ Ⓑ Ⓒ Ⓓ Ⓔ
7 Ⓐ Ⓑ Ⓒ Ⓓ Ⓔ
8 Ⓐ Ⓑ Ⓒ Ⓓ Ⓔ
9 Ⓐ Ⓑ Ⓒ Ⓓ Ⓔ
10 Ⓐ Ⓑ Ⓒ Ⓓ Ⓔ
11 Ⓐ Ⓑ Ⓒ Ⓓ Ⓔ
12 Ⓐ Ⓑ Ⓒ Ⓓ Ⓔ
13 Ⓐ Ⓑ Ⓒ Ⓓ Ⓔ
14 Ⓐ Ⓑ Ⓒ Ⓓ Ⓔ
15 Ⓐ Ⓑ Ⓒ Ⓓ Ⓔ
16 Ⓐ Ⓑ Ⓒ Ⓓ Ⓔ
17 Ⓐ Ⓑ Ⓒ Ⓓ Ⓔ
18 Ⓐ Ⓑ Ⓒ Ⓓ Ⓔ
19 Ⓐ Ⓑ Ⓒ Ⓓ Ⓔ
20 Ⓐ Ⓑ Ⓒ Ⓓ Ⓔ
21 Ⓐ Ⓑ Ⓒ Ⓓ Ⓔ

22 Ⓐ Ⓑ Ⓒ Ⓓ Ⓔ
23 Ⓐ Ⓑ Ⓒ Ⓓ Ⓔ
24 Ⓐ Ⓑ Ⓒ Ⓓ Ⓔ
25 Ⓐ Ⓑ Ⓒ Ⓓ Ⓔ
26 Ⓐ Ⓑ Ⓒ Ⓓ Ⓔ
27 Ⓐ Ⓑ Ⓒ Ⓓ Ⓔ
28 Ⓐ Ⓑ Ⓒ Ⓓ Ⓔ
29 Ⓐ Ⓑ Ⓒ Ⓓ Ⓔ
30 Ⓐ Ⓑ Ⓒ Ⓓ Ⓔ
31 Ⓐ Ⓑ Ⓒ Ⓓ Ⓔ
32 Ⓐ Ⓑ Ⓒ Ⓓ Ⓔ
33 Ⓐ Ⓑ Ⓒ Ⓓ Ⓔ
34 Ⓐ Ⓑ Ⓒ Ⓓ Ⓔ
35 Ⓐ Ⓑ Ⓒ Ⓓ Ⓔ
36 Ⓐ Ⓑ Ⓒ Ⓓ Ⓔ
37 Ⓐ Ⓑ Ⓒ Ⓓ Ⓔ
38 Ⓐ Ⓑ Ⓒ Ⓓ Ⓔ
39 Ⓐ Ⓑ Ⓒ Ⓓ Ⓔ
40 Ⓐ Ⓑ Ⓒ Ⓓ Ⓔ
41 Ⓐ Ⓑ Ⓒ Ⓓ Ⓔ
42 Ⓐ Ⓑ Ⓒ Ⓓ Ⓔ